D1624630

Very Far North

Very Far North

Timothy Murphy

THE WAYWISER PRESS

LONDON
2002

First published in 2002 by

THE WAYWISER PRESS

9 Woodstock Road, London N4 3ET, UK

T: +44 (0)20 8374 5526
F: +44 (0)20 8374 5736

waywiser-press@aol.com
www.waywiser-press.com

Editor
Philip Hoy

A CIP catalogue record for this book is available from the British Library

ISBN 1-904130-01-1

Printed and Bound by

T.J. International Ltd.,
Padstow, Cornwall PL28 8RW, UK

for

Katherine Murphy

It is very far north, we admit, to have brought the peach.

– Robert Frost

Acknowledgements

Thanks to Alan Sullivan for his indispensable editing and for permission to print "Antiquary."

Thanks also to Charlie Beck for letting me reproduce his handsome oak on the cover.

Thanks lastly to editors of the following publications: *The Carolina Quarterly, Chronicles, The Dark Horse, Edge City Review, The Formalist, The Hudson Review, Light, Poetry Daily, The Sewanee Review, Spectrum.*

Several of these poems have appeared in a memoir, *Set the Ploughshare Deep* (Ohio University Press, 2000). Some also appeared in a chapbook, *Tessie's Time* (Fameorshame Press, 1999).

Contents

III. Elsewhere

IV. Red like Him

V. The Visitant

Introduction

In 1996 I was invited by the editor of *The Formalist*, a journal devoted to metrical poetry, to serve as judge for one of their annual competitions, named in honor of Howard Nemerov, and devoted entirely to the sonnet. I was pleased to find more deft and well-crafted poems than I had expected. Nevertheless, I had no difficulty choosing the best of the lot, "The Track of the Storm," headnoted *Bastille Day, 1995*.

> We grieve for the twelve trees we lost last night,
> pillars of our community, old friends
> and confidants dismembered in our sight,
> stripped of their crowns by the unruly winds.
> There were no baskets to receive their heads,
> no women knitting by the guillotines,
> only two sleepers rousted from their beds
> by fusillades of hailstones on the screens.
> Her nest shattered, her battered hatchlings drowned,
> a stunned and silent junco watches me
> chainsawing limbs from corpses of the downed,
> clearing the understorey of debris
> while supple saplings which survived the blast
> lay claim to light and liberty at last.

There was much to be pleased with about this sonnet, and not least was the poet's tact in refusing to allow the poem's donnée – the correspondence of a hailstorm and the French Revolution – to draw him into a mere parade of analogies, and thereby wander too far from the world of chainsaws and juncos (a kind of finch). Only when the winning sonnet appeared in *The Formalist* did I learn the poet's name was Timothy Murphy, a name then totally unknown to me. I wrote to him shortly thereafter to congratulate him, remarking, among other things, "I received a few sullen and envious complaints from other competitors who remained convinced that their poems were better than yours."

That sonnet would, in due course, find its way into Murphy's first book of poems, *The Deed of Gift*, published in 1998, with a preface by Richard Wilbur. Wilbur remains a presiding avatar and embodiment of excellence for Murphy, and in the present book the phrase "invincible desire" is appropriated from Wilbur's untitled sonnet about a scarecrow. Murphy has a number of other literary heroes and mentors, including Robert Penn Warren, his teacher at Yale, as well as poets he never met but venerated, such as Frost, Hardy, and A.D. Hope. These three comprise the cast of characters in a dream he describes in the poem in this book called "The Cortege." He had addressed Hope in an earlier verse epistle:

> Sir, pardon this unheralded address
> From America's outback ...
>
> Like yours my lines and themes were once writ large.
> Alas! my lame pentameters lacked charge.
> Heroic couplets? I abandoned hope,
> dazzled by one man's art, another's scope.
> Dimeter and trimeter I devise
> more skillfully, though slant rhyme is my vice.
> Forewarned (the very word is like a curse)
> please weigh these gleanings from a farmer's verse.

And the poem concludes:

> Though the estate of poetry seems grim,
> young men must hope when prospects look most dim.
> I am your servant and disciple —
>
> *Tim*

It should not be surprising, in a nation as large as America, to find a good deal of regional poetry, regional but not provincial. The South has given us Poe, John Crowe Ransom and Allen Tate, as well as Murphy's teacher, Robert Penn Warren. New England has lavishly supplied three Lowells, along with Longfellow, Whittier, Emerson, Dickinson and Bryant. Things thin out a good deal in "America's Outback," where Murphy farms and writes. Yet if Fargo, North Dakota, seems off the beaten literary track, it has not kept Murphy from the sort

14

of mental voyages abroad that Dickinson liked to make: and in this volume the reader will encounter excursions into Norse Mythology, Inuit legend, Sioux lore, Japanese art, Chinese, Anglo-Saxon, Greek and Latin sources, including a terse condensation of the first choral ode of Sophocles' *Antigone.*

Acknowledging that he feels most at home with short lines ("Dimeter and trimeter"), it must be added that he is also one of the honorable company who favour short poems, a company that includes Martial, Landor, Dickinson, Housman, Yvor Winters, J.V. Cunningham and Robert Francis. In the present volume, "The Abyss" bears a family resemblance to Emily Dickinson in more than its brevity. And though Murphy is not often given to typographical experiment of the kind so deftly employed by May Swenson, one poem here, "Larghetto," is laid out on the page to mimic the geographical drift to the West of the archipelago at the southern tip of Florida where both Frost and Murphy have vacationed.

During the last years of Santayana's life, when he was cared for at the *Clinica della Piccola Compagna di Maria* (the Hospital of the Blue Nuns), the sisters attempted to win the elderly philosopher back to the Catholic faith to which he was born but had long since abandoned. It was said that they discontinued their efforts in this direction when Santayana besought them to pray that his soul, after death, would be permitted to consort with the great pagan philosophers, with Plato, Socrates, Heraclitus, and Democritus. Murphy, in "Poet's Prayer," echoes something like the same sentiment. Yet Murphy's Catholic background, renounced like Santayana's, is in evidence in a number of poems here. As is his Irishness, his wit, his stoic strength and dark, unflinching vision. If his poems are dealt out as morsels, this book constitutes a large, nourishing, and uncommonly varied banquet.

Anthony Hecht

Washington D.C.
August, 2001

15

I. No Place for Trees

No Place For Trees

A few scrub oaks survive
droughts, blizzards, and disease.
Spurge and loosestrife thrive.
This is no place for trees.

Let the returning bison,
gathering like a storm,
darken the bare horizon
of a land unfit to farm.

Headwaters

Up switchbacks to passes
we ride winded horses
through spruces, then grasses
ribboned with watercourses,
the Wind River's sources.

A trail called Highline
meanders through flowers
from treeline to snowline
where War Bonnet glowers
on Cirque of the Towers.

A bald eagle's shadow
plummets from its aerie,
then circles this meadow
whose cold waters carry
some hope to our prairie.

The Last Sodbusters

Wibaux, Montana, 1907

"Rain follows the plough!"
the pamphleteers proclaim.

Does grass follow the cow
or wind, the weathervane?

Care furrows the brow
and bows the straightest frame.

Thistles follow the plough,
and hail threshes the grain.

Bin Buster

The unitrain
departs Lamoure
with surplus grain
for the trading floor,
a laden wain
in a time o' dearth.
Who will remain
to work the earth?

Unposted

Abandoned where the grass grew lank and damp,
the antiquated grain drill seemed a toy
some Lilliputian farmer might employ
to plant a field small as a postage stamp.

Kelly opened a hopper filled with seed
nutty and sweet as Wheaties in the bag.
Where were the ploughman and his plodding nag
to run that good grain through the metered feed?

Flushed from a pigweed patch, a pheasant sailed
over the leafless tree row flecked with red
where shrunken apples hung unharvested
or fallen to the stubble, lay impaled.

Squinting into the distance, Kelly said
"It was the farmer, not the seed what failed."

My Banker

The doctor's daughter and the banker's son
married, and their receivables were joined.
If lending to the poor and sick were one,
oh what a tidy fortune could be coined!

"Mortgage the farm. You'll soon be feeling better,"
they urged the ailing ranchers they encumbered,
and every penny spent by any debtor
was lent by them, collected twice, and numbered.

When Wall Street rated all the country's banks
they graded Morgan first, my banker second,
for which I tender my eternal thanks
but wonder how in Hell his rank is reckoned.

Vulture Acres

He started with half a pasture
and a grove of Soil Bank ash
when farms were selling faster
after a market crash.

He posted "Vulture Acres"
by the dirt track to his shack
on land no other takers
sought at the auction block.

Leasing fields from neighbors
who were old or going broke,
he shouldered barnyard labours
as an ox shoulders a yoke.

He built a cedar smokehouse
where his culled sows were cured
and added a redwood ranch house
when his cash flow was assured.

But he also bought the scripture
that told him all was dust,
however lush the pasture
where someone else went bust.

Country Voices

I. Master Farmer

Corn tassels in July.
On irrigated sand
his crop stands eight feet high,
and corn is in demand.

The picker took my fingers
to fertilize this land.
Only his green thumb lingers.
I shake his other hand.

II. Auction

A slew of buyers came to bid,
their hatbands soaked with sweat.
He bid against some half-baked kid
our banker had never met.
The best damn deals I ever did
was the deals we didn't get.

III. Marksman

She was a face-shot little doe,
her jawbone blown apart.
Her spoor bloodied the early snow.
A hunter hits the heart.

IV. Dollar Corn

Partner, I asked, *How have we sinned?*
Greed in some former life?
Kelly pondered, and then he grinned,
I'd hafta ask the wife.

V. Godfearer

The farmer is a feeder,
a weeder and a waterer,
a husbander, a slaughterer,
and a skillful breeder.

No churchbell in the village
stops him spreading silage
for hungry cows to forage
or halts his April tillage.

He ploughs the powdery plain
while country wives are praying.
His prayer consists of saying,
Now where's the goddamn rain?

The Steward

Lord, thou deliveredst unto me five talents; behold, I have gained five talents more – Matthew XXV, 20

Pheasants and sharptail grouse
nest near his modest house.
Pronghorn antelope
graze on a Rosebud slope.

Morris no-till drills
pulled by three Versatiles
keep the soil from blowing
off his communal hills –

hills that the bison haunted
and his Sioux forbears hunted,
fields where the cocks are crowing
and his green sons, growing.

Dakota Greeting

Frosted sign in a frozen ditch:
Stranger, welcome to Oakes,
home to hundreds of friendly folks
and one mean son-of-a-bitch.

The Honey Wagon

Some say the custom cutters wheeled
   and dealed at his expense.
Some say the aphids ate his yield
   and call it negligence.
Some of the neighbors' lips are sealed –
   the folks with common sense.
You can't fertilize a field
   by farting through the fence.

Blow Winds and Crack Your Cheeks

A stage so large the combine seems a prop:
    the farmer plays by heart
    Tom o' Bedlam's part,
and hail drops like a curtain on the crop.

It Is Very Far North ...

Four giddy days are all that spring allows
the drunken bumblings of our honey bees
before a south wind, stripping petalled boughs,
turns apples into ordinary trees.
Ours have weathered blizzards, freezing rain,
a record flood crest, and a May snow squall.
Now only scab, inchworms, and hail remain
to rob us of an ample apple fall,
a brief lifting of limbs before the snow
grips them with such reluctance to let go.

Next Year, Drought

I. The Frozen Flood

The blizzard hurtles southward
on a river swirling north,
and our oldest farmers say
the Red is not the strongest,
the longest or the broadest
but by God it's the coldest
meanest river in the world.

II. Symphony of a Thousand

I'm listening to Mahler
while students fight all night
to raise the city's dikes.
Decorate them for valor
whether we stand or not
when the crescendo strikes.

III. Going Under

Fargo's victims are weeping
for the people of Grand Forks.
Our steeple bells are pealing
and our believers kneeling,
but nothing stops the seeping,
not Christ or all his clerks.

IV. The Recovery

Thanks for drains and sumps,
for six-inch diesel pumps
and concrete septic tanks,
for neighbors closing ranks
to overcome the flood.
Thanks for our forebears' blood
that still runs in our veins
as rivers vein these plains.

II. Hunters and Prey

Hunters and Prey

And there came a voice to him, "Rise, Peter; kill, and eat." – Acts X, 13

I. Brother Fox

A windless cloudless night
refroze the puddled ice
where geese chose to alight.
Waking at dawn they found
their feet webbed to the pond.
Drawn by their doleful cries
a fox strolled from the wood
with mayhem in his eyes.

II. Whitetails

Hoofed rats that they are,
they live in cervine fear
of carnivores who dine
on tenderloin of deer
or crown rack of fawn
downed with a young red wine.

III. Little Heart Butte

Grouse peck at its breast
and pheasants at its foot.
Buffalo berries west
and Russian olives east
girdle this shortgrass butte,
this table set for a feast.
I, the unbidden guest,
have little heart to shoot.

The Giving of Names

"Why is my elder brother named
    Raven Overhead?"
A raven circled your mother
    when she first came to my bed.

"Why is my elder sister named
    Doe Leaps in the Mist?"
A deer passed in the morning
    while your mother and I kissed.

"Why is my baby sister named
    Star Sets to the West?"
The evening star was sinking
    as I lay on your mother's breast.

"How did you name your younger son?"
    pestered the thumb-sucking
little brave his father called
    Two Dogs Fucking.

Pa Sapa

Lost in a Badlands draw,
I saw the last white buffalo
and leapt up with a startled caw,
transfigured to a crow.
As I flew below Bear Butte,
lightning struck an oak
and split its trunk to the root.
A man stepped from the smoke.
Black Elk spoke:
"These lands your tribe shall keep
so long as grasses grow
and rivers flow.
Your promises were cheap
a hundred years ago.
Restore Pa Sapa to
the disentitled Sioux,
and let me sleep."

The Cook Fire

There is this demon in my lower brain.
Call him the Devil. Call him Charlie Russell.
He guzzles alcohol to dull his pain
and rustles calves beside the Little Mussel.

Why is he pained? Perhaps because the sky
is scared to call the badland its horizon.
Perhaps because a pony on the fly
shies from the shorthorns of a painted bison.

One of the Russells hanging in my head
captures the struggles of a grizzly bear,
twice-roped, spread-eagled, kicking apart a bed
of coals and ashes in his huge despair.

What overcomes insensate fear of fire?
Abandon, or invincible desire?

Color-blind

Hunters agree our labs are black
and see the snow as white,
but lesser hunters simply lack
the Murphy brothers' sight.

Why should greenheads not be red
in the potholes' purple sheen
when the so-called red on a rooster's head
glows like the sunrise, green?

A Gun Dog Named Maud Gonne

She no longer hears
whistle or wings.
The drums in her ears
were delicate things.

There will be water
to gun when she goes,
autumns of slaughter,
winters to doze,
but never a partner
with so sweet a nose.

Spring Cleaning

Their pinions whistle as the pintails fly –
feather dusters brushing an April sky.

Hunting Time

for R. S. Gwynn

It's not just dirt-cheap prices,
diseases in our herds
or the global banking crisis.
Our fields are beset by birds.
Gwynn slips in a cartridge,
and another shell is pinned—
poets and dogs and partridge
all working into the wind.

The raptor is our fellow
predator of the air.
We humans lack his yellow
iris, his slitted stare;
but Brownings are as deadly
as dripping beak or claw,
and our prey bleeds as redly
as rodent eaten raw.

Though nowadays a shooter
keeps impulse under lock,
my old Kentucky tutor
once shot and stuffed a hawk.
He told me time was reckoned
by the crippled bird's last breath
as the marksman spared a second
to practice for his death.

The Recruit

Memorial Day, 1997

An honor guard of battle-scarred old men
discharges antique carbines at the sky
as though the ghosts of war were winging by
like pintails flushing from an ice-rimmed fen.
How many of these troops will hunt next fall?
Fewer and fewer totter out to shoot.
They hardly hear the mallard's bugle call
which lures me to the sloughs with my recruit –
a boy shouldering arms where reeds grow tall
and mankind's present enmities are moot.

Virtual Family

Two foundlings whom we foster
have bedded down together,
each searching for his brother
creature in the tender
features of the other.
Each takes me for his teacher
but sees me as his father
and calls my lover "Mother."

A Marriage

Two glaciers make a river.
The silty water falls.
Is it a troubled mother
or the bouldered bed that calls?
Or is that voice the father?

Freeze-Up

Its great gable flushed
by fading alpenglow,
its frozen gutters hushed
in heather far below,
Denali hunkers crushed
by centuries of snow.
So snow weighs on a shed
or dusts my lover's head.

Henry IV, Part III

A sea fan's fallen leaf
lithifies as a reef
asphyxiates in silt.
Folding and faulting tilt
the ocean's upthrust bed
into a watershed
rivulets trickle down.
Uneasy lies the crown
shells on a misty crest
eloquently attest
before the summits drown.

Specimen Ridge, Alberta

To a Trout

I whet my hook
beneath a pine,
then with a swish
I loft my line
over a brook
of sparkling wine.
Come little fish
and we will dine.

Game Log

"Learn now the lore
of living creatures."
A *clowder* of cats
cheerfully chases
a *charm* of finches,
a *rabble* of robins.
A *shoal* of fishes
frantically flees
a *pod* of seals
or a *gam* of whales.
A *pack* of pointers
flushes from bushes
a *bevy* of quail,
or *covey* of partridge
while hunters are harassed
by *swarms* of hornets,
clouds of mosquitoes,
and *hordes* of wardens.
A *gaggle* of geese
dabble and gabble,
as aimless as auks
or a *plague* of poets.

Eidyllion

I am selling my farms
to build a butterfly barn
where multicolored swarms
will storm the glassy dome
to greet the midnight sun,
and that will be my home.

III. ELSEWHERE

Elsewhere

A goose in the yard yearns for a barn,
and the penned bird, to go free.
The returning salmon yearns for the tarn
from which its fry will flee.

Elsewhere ... what is its lasting charm
for the creature in misery?
A fisherman longs for the land-locked farm
its tenant would trade for the sea.

Homecoming

I found fierce dogs
guarding my pens
and fattened hogs
behind each fence.
Six hundred sows
fed the swine
who thronged my house
and swilled my wine.

I found a son
too green to draw
my bow of yew,
a queen who saw
her work undone,
her scullions too.
For *this* I quit
Circe's arms –
a manumit
to stinking farms?

A seer I trust
told me in Hell
how I could quell
my wanderlust:
"Go seek a man
so far inland
from Poseidon's shore
he'll think the oar
you bear in hand
a winnowing fan."

The Wanderer

There is no end
        to a wanderer's sorrow.
The wisdom of Erda
        queried by Wotan,
the counsel of Ragna
        sung in a saga
I'll follow tomorrow –
        tomorrow if ever –
for I am no friend
        of Volsung or Vala.

The Talisman

"Summer was longer,
        the sun warmer
when the barley-eaters
        built their barrows,"
said the seal-stalker,
        toothlessly smiling.
"*Godhavn*, their helmsmen
        named this harbor
when longboats rode
        over open water.
As for the raven,
        they called him *hrefn*.
I eat bone marrow,
        blood and whale meat,
so I know nothing
        but names for snow."

In a tattered tent
       the red-haired trekker
stared at the soapstone
       unwrapped from a rag.
Bear cubs basked
       on a blue whale's back
and salmon soared
       over a skua.
Hewn by the hand
       of an idle hunter,
narwhals twined
       with the Talelayo
whose severed fingers
       fluttered like fishes
or dreams drawn
       from the depths of a stone.

The Aerie

Hand-laid cables of braided twine
anchored a Boy Scout monkey bridge.
Over it rose an aspen ridge
where ospreys hunched on a blasted pine.

Ever a student of their flight,
I've envied them the breakneck plunge,
the snatched fish and the skyward lunge
from Bad Axe Lake to Key West Bight.

An osprey perched on the foremast
of a tall schooner berthed near mine
watches me cinch a slack springline.
So the familiars of my past
accepted an ungainly guest
and fledged a sailor from their nest.

Landfall

We skirt a squall to windward
    and shelter on our lee,
but the sure passage inward
    is reefed so cunningly
mariners pray for sunshine
    to light their briny way
over the coral-crusted chine
    of this uncharted bay.

If skippers had their wishes
    passages would be brief,
cannons would not house fishes
    on galleons come to grief,
headlands would remain in sight,
    and lamps brightly burning
would signal vessels in the night
    red right returning.

Helming All Night

Spelling a reprobate
whose compass heading veers,
my first mate and last mate
stares at the stars and steers.

The Watch

When I leave this little ship
(which I can ill-afford)
spring-lined in a slip,
I leave my love aboard.

If the weather is in doubt
he scans the sky for signs.
When the spring tide runs out,
love will adjust my lines.

Doldrums

Becalmed on the Sargasso sea,
I feared my crew would mutiny.
With half the deckhands on report,
water and rum, running short,
I passed the word. My bosun roared,
"Heave the horses overboard."

Mr. Christian's Diary

Our vessel is a venue
where injustice swiftly moves.
"The floggings will continue
until the morale improves."

Lemuel's Travels

I am a slender note
rolled in a stoppered flask.
Year after year I float
wherever currents lead me,
and everywhere I ask
Who in the world will read me?

Note in a Bottle

We row, row in the benches
to pull our galley free
from three winged wenches
who sing, sing by the sea.

Larghetto

                                   From
                                   Key Biscayne
                                   the islands
                                   trend

                                   southwest
                                   in a leeward
                                   bend

                              until they end
                         where Robert Frost

                    quarrelled
            with the world

   and lost.

Sea Grapes

Sodden, he drifts ashore
like a worm-ridden spar
or broken-bladed oar
hung in a beachfront bar.

Virgin church bells peal
and the parched pastors preach
while feral piglets squeal
for fruit they cannot reach.

Second-in-Command

Freed by a shift of wind
after running aground,
a ship shorn of its rudder
rigged a fothering sail
under its injured keel.
A son mourning his skipper
stood at the useless wheel.

IV. RED LIKE HIM

Red Like Him

for Robert Penn Warren

He was tutor to a lad
he never really knew –
only the shock of red
like sunrise on a slough.

Out for an autumn walk,
I hear the great geese cry
and hail a red-tailed hawk
spiralling up the sky.

Mentor

for Robert Francis

Had I known, only known
when I lived so near,
I'd have gone, gladly gone
foregoing my fear
of the wholly grown
and the nearly great.
But I learned alone,
so I learned too late.

Collateral

"Go home, boy. Buy a farm.
Sink your toes in that rich soil
and grow yourself some roots."
No stranger to the toil
of those who raise their fruits,
he clasped my freckled arm
and dragged me down to earth.
I learned to measure worth
as the plough measures a furrow.
Calling on country banks,
I pledge, encumber, borrow
and tell a dead man, "Thanks."

Boom and Bust

i.m. Gordon Cook

An old man with a wink:
"I struck it rich three times.
Whenever I was broke
bellhops tipped their caps,
beggars took my dimes
and maitre d's, our wraps.
What did my Ida lack?
In fat years and in lean,
I had good scotch to drink,
Cuban cigars to smoke,
and fine wool on my back.
So what does money mean?"

Horses for my Father

I. Alexander's Cavalry

Horses at Chaeronea
trampled the Theban Band.
Later at Gaugamela
where Persia made its stand,
horses embarrassed Darius
with flanking incursions,
harassing his chariots
and myriads of Persians.

II. Two Metaphors

Someone described the horse
as "poetry in motion."
Another beside the ocean
saw "horses of the sea."
The latter phrase has force,
but I dispute the notion
that horses are poetry –
it's not fair to the horse.

III. Montana *Koan*

Two fillies on the plains –
was it their flowing manes
or was it the wind that flew?
The twisted sage maintains
It was the mind that blew.

IV. The Cutting

Culled from a milling herd
a calf bawls at the sky,
and heifers question why
ponies were ever spurred.

Cowboy, colt and calf
all with their tails awry –
as though my dogs and I
ran roosters through the chaff

and made the feathers fly.

V. Look Homeward, Rancher

Riding to Beartooth Pass
he looks back at the plains,
ranges of grazed-out grass
thirsting for mountain rains –

a bankrupt watershed
where ledgers testify
that black ink runs red
after the stock ponds dry.

VI. Put to Pasture

The old stud is grazing,
nickering and lazing
near the knacker's yard.

He's shucked off all traces
of dirt-track races
scored on a loser's card.

What bookie has the greed
to handicap a steed
when it has run so hard?

VII. My Father Young and Old

Ancient writers say three score years and ten
are all the time the gods allotted men.
Don't tell that to my father in his eighties
whom Cerberus has yet to greet in Hades.

Spending his boyhood on a horse-drawn plough
gained him the furrows on his worried brow,
the music in his dimming memories:
"chain tugs ringing on the steel singletrees."

VIII. Transformation

The old stallion dies.
Our roan no longer roams
beneath our outsized skies.
In a gorge loud with streams
beyond the Great Divide,
an eagle blinds a hare,
rips the heart from its side,
and bears it to his lair.

IX. Lines from the *Antigone*

The wonders of this world are numberless,
but none of them more wonderful than man
who broke the spirit of the mountain bull,
yoking its lathered shoulders to his plough.
He saddled the wild stallion, windy-maned,
and rode the ocean with his plunging prow.
All creatures of the sea and earth he named,
taming them with the nets cast by his mind,
and yet – against the forces of one wind,
the last tempest of death, he cannot stand.

Tessie's Talk

She called our county drain *The Burn*
when I was *wee* and she was worn.
At the field's edge she built a *cairn*:
"Rags on a scarecrow *ward* the corn."

While darning socks with worsted *yearne*
or *milching coos* in a hip-roofed barn,
she sang Burns to a jug-eared *bairn*.
A *ferlie* whirled in her butter churn.

Tessie's Time

She said the sundial stood so long
because it only counted hours
    when the sun was shining.

Its daily lesson kept her strong,
showing her how to husband powers
    despite their slow declining.

When the years totaled ninety-one,
    she was thirty-nine by the sun.

The Pallbearers

At the prairie cemetery
where the river meets a road
and Murphys come to bury
love in the loam we've sowed
my brother lets me carry
the light end of the load.

Dies Irae

At the field's edge a feather
clings briefly to a bough
before a change of weather
offers it to the plough,
much as it did my father.

Pater Vincit Omnia

Vincere means *to vanquish*.
His last words to a son
and daughters in his anguish
made light of the Latin language:
he smiled and said, "Vince won."

From the Neck Up

An old farmer said: "Hjalmer!
Are you in town today too?
I yust can't remember
was it your brudder or you
who died last December?"

My brother and I remember
that mud-tracked saloon
as Dad's doddering partner
asks, "Will Vince be home soon?"

The Cortege

Last night I dreamed that A.D. Hope was dead.
Thomas Hardy was riding on the hearse
as Frost strolled slowly by the horse's head.
"His judgments were as measured as his verse,"
the elder of those two "proud songsters" said.

The horse had no idea whom he was towing;
no mourners lined the silent streets they crossed.
"His *Western Elegies* rival *The Going,*
and though I grant it grudgingly," said Frost,
"his *Hay Fever* is better than my *Mowing.*"

V. THE VISITANT

The Visitant

for Suzanne Doyle

When last this comet crossed the West
Sappho lay on her lover's breast.
How I'd have loved to hear her speak
its praises in Aeolic Greek,
mankind's most majestic tongue
for which Apollo's lyre was strung.
When next this astral visitant
returns from its celestial jaunt,
will jewels in Berenice's Hair
still shine above a planet where
lovers observe a comet's flight
then light a votive lamp to write
strophes a poet might have sung
when Sappho and the Gods were young?

Mirkwood

No sunlight pierced the forest's warp and woof,
though raindrops dribbled through its leaky roof
while widow-makers tottered in the gloom
and spiders lured butterflies to their doom.

Faintly I heard a silver thread of sound –
water or laughter. Following it I found
nine mushrooms nodding in a fairy ring
and a black viceroy hung from a silken string.

What numbing toxin does a dream secrete
before it twists me in a winding sheet?
When I least understand my darkest dread
I think there are most spiders in my bed.

Flight across the Moor

I dreamt I was a knight
prostrated by my grief
and torn by disbelief
no chalice could set straight.

I staggered across a moor
where white wolves were stocked
and finally reached a tower
only to find it locked.
An owl flew widdershins
around its crumbling crown,
hooting for all the sins
my guilty flesh had borne.
I fished a crooked pin
out of my twisted pocket.
This was no wayside inn
but a wolf-guarded tower
with an ensorcelled door,
and I could not unlock it.

I had become a cur
whom the encircling wolves
which are my nightmare selves
dismembered on the moor.

Methuselah

Our Bronco bucked on rocks as daybreak's glow
drove darkness down the range from summit snow.
We rode to where the switchback track was blocked;
        and then we walked
into a world where strings were not yet strung
on tortoise shells, where Gilgamesh was young.
No epic in an unsung tongue would mark
        our Patriarch.
A jay betrayed him, hopping from a boulder
to screech "Here!" on his desiccated shoulder.
One limb was green. Needled and thinly skinned,
        it whipped the wind.
He stood rooted beneath a slide of shale,
but over his head a snowfield filled its sail
as though to float him back across the years
        on Uruk's tears.

Lines Written in Bondage

I am no man of letters,
only a puppet on a string
dancing jerkily in my fetters
when I hear my betters sing.

Lines Written in Homage

I cannot quite abolish
the follies of my youth
or forge the English language
with the plangent ring of truth
Borges brings to Spanish,
so let me hush my anguish
with a whisper of vermouth.

Casa Abandonada

for Robert Mezey

Though he labours in the shadows,
the library of his mind
is a corridor of windows
whose occupant is blind.

The manse is Argentina
but a mirror gives on Spain
as a gaucho's ocarina
moans through a broken pane.

Cobwebs trail from ceilings
over lovers and their bowers.
Mice run on the railings;
a cracked clock-face glowers.

Fingering newel or plinth,
the blind man cannot see
his way through this labyrinth.
Neither, my friend, can we.

Allegory

If a little cassowary
hatched in an ossuary
that would be a very
scary sort of aerie
for a wary cassowary.

Antiquary

Pity the flitting fritillary
fluttering in a library.
He's apt to be a very
frayed and solitary
literary fritillary.

by Alan Sullivan

Poet's Prayer

When I die and go to hell,
as I most certainly shall
(being such an unbeliever)
good Lord, please deliver
my soul to that shady dell
where the pagan poets dwell.
And there, Lord, let me seek
masters of trope and rhyme –
the infernal and the sublime –
and toil until the end of time
to learn Latin and Greek.

The Making of an Artist

After the War, an unnamed Oxford don,
a soldier then, seduced a Roman boy
in a brief flurry of paedophilic joy,
but woke one day to find his minion gone.

The don, shamed by his momentary rage,
consoled himself with academic fame,
and publishing his monograph, became
the foremost lepidopterist of his age.

Years later, at a gathering in France,
the don spotted a face he surely knew
and blurted: "Franco, darling! Is it you?"
The great director looked at him askance:

"I'm sorry, but your name has slipped my mind.
There were so many, and they were all so kind."

Il Poverello

Leaving Giotto's frescoed nave,
I climbed from the foothill town
to see the saint's unpainted cave
where Satan was cast down.

The cleft on Mount Subasio
was perilous and wooded,
and the young monk from Gubbio
beautiful but hooded.

He smiled like an angel kissed,
kissed by Giotto's tincture.
Beads were twisted round his wrist;
his waist, bound in a cincture.

He whispered *"Vade retro"*
when the Devil came to parley
and prayed, prayed from *l'Eremo*
for the songbirds and the barley.

Apologia Pro Ecclesia Sua

Holy Father, you slip a folded prayer
between two stone blocks at the Wailing Wall.
What do you pray for? An end to the despair
that holds the land of Palestine in thrall?

Your sermon is an overdue endeavor
to make your peace with women, Muslims, Jews.
But not with homosexuals. No, never.
Ours is the priestly sin you won't excuse.

Crippled by your incurable disease,
you shuffle slowly through the Holy Land
as throngs of sinners praying on their knees
bow to the scepter in your palsied hand.

You preach that God is three and God is one?
If He exists, you are His dying son.

Four Sorrows

Seed carelessly planted,
fair counsel rejected,
love taken for granted
and Sappho uncollected.

Post Mortem

A certain erratic
erotic erratum
was found at the bottom
of Timothy's attic,
or was it his closet?

The Abyss

His subterfuge is deep
and devious is his task,
but the man behind the mask
I take off when I sleep
is the one friend I can ask
to look before I leap.

The Cask Master

He keeps his whiskey flask
hidden from partners' eyes.
Sworn to a sober task,
he mouths his sodden lies.
His is a wooden mask –
a visage veined and mottled –
aged like the oaken cask
from which his oaths are bottled.

The Dead Poet

At last the path runs straight
from his hovel to the skies
and the bolted postern gate
of the Western Paradise
where seven times seven
Immortals judge a throng,
admitting some to heaven
for the pittance of a song.

The Muromachi Cranes

With outstretched wings the dancers pirouette.
Arching graceful necks
they open great green beaks
and join their voices in a wild duet.

Preening and strutting on a silken stage
the cranes are not dismayed
that painted feathers fade.
Immortals grow more ravishing with age.

Contentedly they wade the swirling ink
of their appointed pool
where spawning minnows school
and poets are prohibited to drink.

As the sun sets on snow peaks in the West
snow cranes contemplate
the chirps which emanate
from the lone egg sequestered in their nest.

Over that egg a four-toed foot is curled
as though a Taoist sage
in a thatched hermitage
slowly revolves the ovum of the world.

The Drowned Immortal

When an Immortal misbehaves,
his penance is to live with men
until, reborn among their graves,
he dies to join the gods again.

One such soul was called Li Po.
Too whimsical for palace life,
the poet roved, *incognito*,
unfettered by a son or wife.

Spurning the aristocracy,
he traipsed tipsily through the South
and left his deathless poetry
to grace many a drunkard's mouth.

One night, teaching the moon to sing,
he bent close to her mirrored face.
The jealous river, listening,
gathered him in her chill embrace.

The Sixth Dalai Lama

I picture him in purple silk *de Chine*,
his perfumed locks voluptuously long.
Singing a favorite his latest song,
Tsangyang Gyatso, poet and libertine,
dismissed the cares of Buddhahood and State,
the tedium of rituals and texts.

Far from the palace and its scheming sects,
the brothel-keepers called him "Profligate"
and "Man of Many Loves." The girls believed
his Tantric mastery enhanced orgasms,
uniting Yin with Yang in cosmic spasms
whereby Transcendent Insight was achieved.

Neglecting to defend the Land of Snows,
he kowtowed for the Manchu Emperor
who lured him to confer at Gunga Nor
and left his corpse to edify the crows.

The Collector

Breaching the Great Wall, a superior force
routed the armies of the Northern Sung.
South sped the beaten Emperor, Hui Tzung;
hard at his heels, a hundred thousand horse.

Stragglers staggered into his bivouac,
too feeble and too few to reengage.
He bore the loss of Empire like a sage
but blanched when he was told about the sack.

Filigreed jades and priceless porcelains,
his famed collection of calligraphy,
Li Po's and Tu Fu's deathless poetry –
pilfered by gibbering barbarians?

Travel, he loathed; poverty, he abhorred.
Surely the Khan could spare a small estate.
Hui Tzung meekly submitted to his fate,
a lacquered bauble for the Mongol hoard.

Bad Karma

A girl driving her donkeys out to grass
was ambushed by an old, outlandish man
who tried to straddle her. The robust lass
thrust off her would-be ravisher and ran
home to her mother in their humble yurt.
As barking mastiffs spooked her father's yak,
the lathered girl had scarcely breath to blurt
her story of the reprobate's attack.

Her mother recognized the Tantric seer
Dugpa Kunlegs, revered throughout Tibet.
Among the Nyingmapa he had no peer;
who knew what prodigy he might beget?
"Go throw your body at his sacred feet
and gratify the mighty lama's whim,"
mother instructed daughter. "Go entreat
Rinpoche's pardon for repulsing him!"

The girl returned and flung herself prostrate.
"My child," the Holy One sighed wearily,
"Women don't interest me. You've come too late
to implement my purpose. Recently
the Grand Lama of Yerpa Gompa died.
Wasting his life on drunkenness and mirth,
he left a host of sins unrectified.
I sought to save him from a bad rebirth
after I glimpsed his spirit drifting here.
But while you left your herd to graze, alas,
two of your donkeys coupled; and I fear
the Grand Lama will be reborn an ass."

Timing

Walking a narrow path
where pilgrims go astray,
I regulate my breath
because I cannot pray.

So many avatars
have trudged harder ways:
we call them Boddhisatvas,
the saints whom sinners praise.

Contemplating anguish
(which I confuse with sin)
I struggle to extinguish
its mortal origin.

Whether they come from China,
Qom or Bethlehem,
or teach in Dharamsala,
come, let us walk with them.

I labour on the path
because the path is climbing,
leading beyond my death
and its uncertain timing.

Prayer to Milarepa

Your master Marpa
was a humble farmer
but a mighty lama
tutored by Naropa.
He spread the Dharma
from Chomolungma
to the Vale of Lhasa.

Holy Milarepa,
I know no mantra
to correct my karma.
Teach me the tantra.
Translate a farmer
to far Shambala
or perhaps, Nirvana.

Notes

21   The Last Sodbusters: I owe this poem to *Badland,* by Jonathan Raban.

28   The Steward: is South Dakota farmer William Huber. No-till drills inject seed into old stubble, reducing soil erosion. Morris and Versatile are equipment manufacturers.

29   The Honey Wagon: a manure spreader.

38   *Pa Sapa*: Sioux name for the Black Hills.

39   The Cook Fire: C.M. Russell was a Montana artist who died of alcoholism in 1926.

50   *Eidyllion*: a brief lyric on a rustic theme.

54   Homecoming: the fate of Odysseus as prophesied by Tiresias.

55   The Wanderer: Erda is an earth goddess; Wotan, king of the gods in Norse mythology. Ragna is a wise woman in the *Orkneyaman's Saga*. The Volsung are a race of heroes, and the Vala are the gods.

56   The Talisman: Talelayo is a sea goddess of Inuit legend. Severed in a fight, her fingers became fishes.

59   Landfall: *Red right returning* is a sailor's mnemonic. Skippers who are not color-blind leave red buoys to starboard when returning to land.

62   Lemuel's Travels: Published accounts of voyages by Captain Lemuel Gulliver inspired Jonathan Swift to write his satirical classic.

63 *Larghetto*: a play on a musical term and Key Largo. Robert Frost wintered in Key West and composed this epitaph: "He had a lover's quarrel with the world."

77 *Pater Vincit Omnia*: means "Father conquers all."

84 Methuselah: is 4,700 years old and lives in the Inyo Forest's Bristlecone Pine Sanctuary. This poem is dedicated to Anthony Hecht, who is reputedly younger.

90 *Il Poverello*: means "the little poor one," a folk name for Saint Francis, whose hermitage, *l'Eremo*, was located on Mount Subasio above Assisi. *Vade retro* means "get thee behind me," a traditional charm to avert temptation.

91 *Apologia Pro Ecclesia Sua*: means "apology for his church."

95 The Muromachi Cranes: a scroll painted in the Muromachi period of Japanese art, circa 1570-1610.

99 Bad Karma: *Nyingmapa* were a sect known for magical practices. *Rinpoche* is an honorific applied to a high lama. A *gompa* is a lamasery. *The Drowned Immortal, The Collector, Bad Karma,* and *The Sixth Dalai Lama* date from the 1970s and were revised for inclusion here.

101 Prayer to Milarepa: the three teachers named in this poem lived circa the Twelfth Century. Chomolungma is the Tibetan name for Mount Everest. Shambala (Shangri-la) is a mythic vale where the elect are reborn.

Index of Titles and First Lines

A Note About The Author

Timothy Murphy (b.1951) was graduated from Yale in 1972 as Scholar of the House in Poetry. His tutor was Robert Penn Warren.

The Deed Of Gift (Story Line Press, 1998) collects Murphy's poems from 1976 to 1996. *Set The Ploughshare Deep* (Ohio University Press, 2000) is a memoir in prose and verse which recounts his experiences farming and hunting the high plains.

A verse translation of *Beowulf*, on which he collaborated with his partner, Alan Sullivan, will be included in the Longman Anthology of British Literature and be published by Longman as a critical edition in July of 2002.

When he was 21, Mr. Warren told him: "Go home, boy. Buy a farm. Sink your toes in that rich soil and grow some roots."

Murphy is now the managing partner of Timco Farms, Murphy Brothers Farms, Orchard Glen Development Company, and Bell Properties.

He is a director and founder of Bell Farms LLP, Speedy Rake LLC, and Bytespeed LLC. He is President of V.R. Murphy and Sons, Inc., which provides "venture capital" to the aforementioned farming and manufacturing companies.